W9-DJH-149

COUNTRY

Vol. 46, No. 4

Publisher, Patricia A. Pingry
Executive Editor, Cynthia Wyatt
Art Director, Patrick McRae
Production Manager, Jeff Wyatt
Editorial Assistant, Kathleen Gilbert
Copy Editors, Marian Hollyday
              Rhonda Colburn

ISBN 0-8249-1074-5

IDEALS—Vol. 46, No. 4 June 1989 IDEALS (ISSN 0019-137X) is published eight times a year: February, March, May, June, August, September, November, December by IDEALS PUBLISHING CORPORATION, Nelson Place at Elm Hill Pike, Nashville, Tenn. 37214. Second class postage paid at Nashville, Tennessee, and additional mailing offices. Copyright © 1989 by IDEALS PUBLISHING CORPORATION. POSTMASTER: Send address changes to Ideals, Post Office Box 148000, Nashville, Tenn. 37214-8000. All rights reserved. Title IDEALS registered U.S. Patent Office.

SINGLE ISSUE—$3.95
ONE-YEAR SUBSCRIPTION—eight consecutive issues as published—$17.95
TWO-YEAR SUBSCRIPTION—sixteen consecutive issues as published—$31.95
Outside U.S.A., add $6.00 per subscription year for postage and handling.

ACKNOWLEDGMENTS

A BIRD CAME DOWN THE WALK by Emily Dickinson was reprinted by permission of the publishers and the Trustees of Amherst College from THE POEMS OF EMILY DICKINSON, edited by Thomas H. Johnson, Cambridge, Mass.: The Belknap Press of Harvard University Press, Copyright 1951, © 1955, 1979, 1983 by The President and Fellows of Harvard College; NO HONEY-GATHERER from the HARBOR LIGHTS OF HOME by Edgar A. Guest, Copyright 1928 by The Reilly & Lee Co. Used by permission of the Estate; THE CRICKET by Frederick Goddard Tuckerman was first printed in 1954 at the Cummington Press in Omaha, NE. Reprinted in THE COMPLETE POEMS OF FREDERICK GODDARD TUCKERMAN, edited by N. Scott Momaday; Copyright 1965 by Oxford University Press, Inc. Reprinted by permission. Our sincere thanks to the following whose addresses we were unable to locate: Mary Carlier for THE SILENT SONGS; the Estate of Alice B. Dorland for THE FARM; the Estate of Glenn Ward Dresbach for THE BROWN COLT from THE COLLECTED POEMS, 1914-1948, OF GLENN WARD DRESBACH (Caxton, 1950); Alma Eymann for GRANDMA'S GARDEN; George W. Goretzke for TIGER LILIES; John C. Karrer for SUMMER JOY; Hilda M. Krohn for A CARNATION FOR YOU; Wanda J. Wright for RED BEANS AND CORN BREAD.

Front and back covers
ORANGE COUNTY, VERMONT
Dick Dietrich

Photo Opposite
DAISY CHRYSANTHEMUMS
Bob Taylor

Wild Roses

Hilda Sanderson

Wild roses on an arbored fence
    Or on a hillside slope
Remind me of a simpler time,
    When we were all plain folk.

Too busy for much gardening,
    Except for table fare,
We cherished pretty things that grew
    With very little care.
Wild roses volunteered their blooms
    In generous display—
Their robust branches climbed and spread
    Their glorious array.

And even now they are to me
    A special part of June . . .
Old-fashioned beauty every year—
    A busy gardener's boon!

Photo Opposite
A ROSY WELCOME
CRAFTSBURY COMMON
VERMONT
Dick Dietrich

Grandma's Garden

Alma Eymann

Grandma's garden was a rainbow
Of larkspurs, pinks, and phlox;
And the picket gates were guarded
By flaming hollyhocks.
Parasols of poppies fluttered
Scarlet in the breeze;
And splendid, showy orchis peeped
Round garden balsam's knees.
Sweet peas wore silk bonnets,
And snapdragons' velvet jaws
Snapped at children's fingers
In that garden of Grandma's.

There was lacy dill for pickles,
Pungent sage to flavor meat,
And lavender and rosemary
To keep her linens sweet.
There was calico sweet william
And the pansy's faint perfume;
The yucca swung his dagger,
And the sweet sultan his broom.
Grandma had such lovely roses,
And her big Harrison's gold
Filled the long June days with sunshine
In those happy days of old.

She battled bugs with soapsuds,
Planted castor beans for moles,
And trained Kentucky snap beans
On rustic, tented poles.
Grandma simply never heard
Of garden clubs and such,
And she didn't go for harmony
In color very much;
But no formal plot of rare design
Could hold more joy, I know,
Than that patchwork garden of Grandma's
In the days of long ago.

The Ragged Regiment

Alice Williams Brotherton

I love the ragged veterans of June,
Not your trim troop drill-marshaled for display
In gardens fine—but such as dare the noon
With saucy faces by the public way:

Moth mullein with its moth wing petals bright,
Round dandelion, and twining sweet pea vine,
The golden butter-and-eggs, and oxeye white,
Wild parsley, milkweed, and blue columbine.

Ha, sturdy tramps of nature, mustered out
From garden service, scorned, and set apart—
There's not one member of your ragged rout
But makes a warmth of welcome in my heart.

Photo Opposite
FLOWERING SWEET PEA
PORT OXFORD, OREGON
Ed Cooper Photography

Tiger Lilies!

George W. Goretzke

Nodding suddenly before me,
  Tiger lilies in the sun,
By an overgrown country fencerow
  Where the quail and rabbits run.
Through a garden gate half-fallen,
  Mid grapevines and in tangled weeds—
And a bygone joy aroused me
  To follow where the pathway leads!

Winding through the tiger lilies,
  With the mist before my eyes,
To a weather-beaten cottage
  Out beneath the timeless skies—
Blue above the peaceful clearing,
  Blue above the days gone by,
Where the tiger lilies listened
  To the twilight's lullaby.

I remembered other gardens
  And a boy so young and fair—
The ripened prairie wheat straw
  Placed the gold glint in his hair!
When his heart was like the lilies—
  Wild but nearer heaven,
It led him through the sunrise . . .
  Oblivious to ways of men.

Tiger lilies down the pathway
  Where old fancies lightly run,
Peek at me through the old fencerow,
  Out toward the setting sun.
Spilling golden thoughts at nightfall
  Round a clearing in the wood;
Tiger lilies nod gently near me
  Like they really understood!

Photo Opposite
DAYLILIES
LANCASTER, PENNSYLVANIA
Lefever/Grushow
Grant Heilman Photography, Inc.

Summer Joy

John C. Karrer

To walk upon a sun-touched beach
Ankle deep in rolling surf
And watch the sea gulls soar;
To dodge the children as they splash
Along the water's edge
And play a kind of hide-and-seek
With castles on the shore;

To run and take a cooling plunge
Into the blue-green waves,
While little shells and living things
Are tossed beneath your feet;
To feast one's eyes upon the boats
Which sail just out of reach
And see them as they run flat-out
Up and down the fleet;

To find small stones and glass which, now,
Are smooth from nature's touch
And gather different shapes and types
Of lovely drifted wood;
To watch the kites fly up the sky
Then plummet toward the earth,
As treasure hunters, unaware,
Dig for things of worth:

These are moments to be savored
As they come our way;
They can give us so much pleasure—
These joys of summer days.

Photo Overleaf
BOUNTIFUL LUPINES
H. Armstrong Roberts, Inc.

Photo Opposite
FLORAL VISTA
HUMBUG MOUNTAIN BEACH
OREGON
Ed Cooper Photography

BACK IN THE BAY

Zenith Hess

Today I must let the day unwind
Its silken skein from my weary mind;
Just let the summer breeze lazily play,
While minutes and hours slide softly away
Like beads from a necklace, scattered around,
Searched for but not to ever be found.

My boat will carry me back in the bay
Where sunshine sparkles on ripples at play,
Where a stray breeze ruffles the lotus' green skirt,
And the heron gives out a raucous alert
As I approach to spoil his daily fishing,
And I reach the spot for which I've been wishing.

I drop my line by a weathered, old tree
That leans far out, its reflection to see.
A canny, green turtle drops off with a splash,
And a wily, brown muskrat makes a wild dash
For his home down under roots mossy and gray.
He's hoping that I haven't moved in to stay.

I sit and I dream, warmed by the sun;
Troubles slip away silently, one by one.
Then a jerk on my pole! I was dreaming, alas,
And gave a fine minnow to a greedy old bass.
I bait up my hook and again drop my line.
(I hope he enjoyed his dinner just fine!)

Again there's a jerk. This time I'm awake.
I reel in—and just then I see him break
The water and valiantly fight to get free
As he takes one last look at his home 'neath the tree.
I dislodge the hook and admire his beauty—
Then free him; I feel that he's done his duty.

So the day passes with nature's sweet pleasures;
And in memory's chest I'm storing up treasures
To be savored again and again on the morrow
When the world will demand. I'll be able to borrow
The feeling of peace and contentment I found
Way back in the bay when tomorrow comes round.

CRAFTWORKS

Sunbonnet Sue Pillow

The Sunbonnet Sue pattern featured on these pillows by Darlene Kronschnabel has been prominent in the American quilt-making tradition for generations. These pillows are easy to assemble and lend an authentic country touch to a room. Directions for making these lovely pillows follow on the next two pages.

Materials Needed:

1¼ yards 45-inch calico fabric for pillow backing and ruffle

½ yard unbleached muslin for pillow front
  Scissors
  White or brown wrapping paper for pattern
  Ruler
  Sandpaper *or* heavy cardboard for pattern
  Pencil

¼ yard solid-color cotton for bonnet, arms, and legs

¼ yard cotton print for dress
  Straight pins

1 3-inch piece lace or ribbon for bonnet

2 yards off-white eyelet lace for edging around pillow

1 14-inch square pillow form

Photo Opposite
Gerald Koser

Step One: Cutting Material From Pattern

From calico cut three 7 × 45-inch strips for ruffle; then cut one 15 × 15-inch square for the pillow backing. From the muslin cut one 15 × 15-inch square for the pillow front.

To enlarge the pattern, use a large sheet of wrapping paper and rule off 1-inch squares. Make sure you rule off as many squares as the diagram shows. Then draw in the same lines as in each corresponding square of the diagram. Cut out pattern pieces. Transfer individual pieces to either sandpaper or cardboard. Cut out each pattern piece exactly for a perfect fit.

Place the pieces on the wrong side of fabric and carefully trace around each piece with a soft lead pencil. Cut out material.

Step Two: Stitching Patchwork

Fold muslin square in quarters and finger press to determine center. Place pins on the markings at the edge of square. Arrange pattern pieces according to number on the front of the muslin. To hold in place for stitching, baste, pin, or glue using small dots of glue stick. With the widest zigzag stitch and a small stitch length setting, stitch piece number 1, then 2, and so on. Edge the bonnet with lace or ribbon when all pieces are stitched in place.

Step Three: Preparing Ruffle

Place ends of ruffle strips together; stitch to make one continous loop of fabric. Fold this loop in half

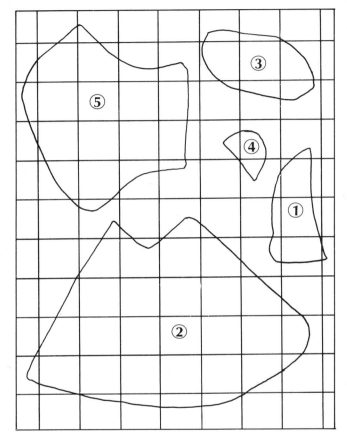

lengthwise with *wrong* sides together. Divide the fabric length into fourths and mark these points with pins on folded edge.

Between one section of markers, machine baste ¼ inch and ⅜ inch from raw edge. Stop each row of stitching at pin markers. Cut thread and tie knot on one end. Repeat for other sections.

Step Four: Sewing Ruffle to Pillow Front

Beginning in center of one side of pillow front, baste eyelet lace to pillow front with right sides together. Leave about 1½ inches of eyelet extending beyond basting at beginning and end. Be sure to allow extra fullness at the corners by taking little pleats, using about 1½ inches at each corner.

Pin ruffle to the pillow front over the eyelet, matching raw edges of the ruffle and pillow. Also match the pins in the ruffle and the pillow edge.

Draw up the gathering threads on the ruffle to fit the pillow front. Space the gathers evenly and allow extra fullness at the corners. Sew the ruffle to the pillow front with a ½-inch seam allowance. Check to be sure the eyelet and ruffle are not caught at the corners or any other place, but do not press open.

Step Five: Finishing Pillow

With right sides together, pin pillow back to front, keeping the eyelet and ruffle flat against the pillow front as you join the two. Sew on three sides and stitch in 1¼ inches on both ends of the fourth side. Trim seams and corners and remove basting. Turn pillow to right side and position pillow form inside.

To close, turn under seam allowance on open side and pin in the middle. Center pins to left and right every ½ inch. Close opening with a blind stitch.

Darlene Kronschnabel

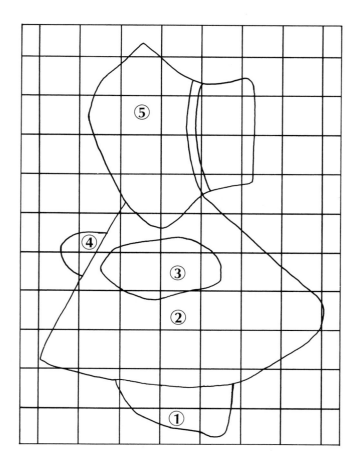

Darlene Kronschnabel is a frequent contributor to Ideals *and other national publications and has shared many lovely craft projects with us. She is also the author of five cookbooks published by Ideals Publishing Corporation. She designed these sunbonnet girl pillows especially for her granddaughters who live in Missouri. Darlene lives, writes, cooks, and sews in Depere, Wisconsin.*

Country Muffins

Apricot Walnut Muffins

Makes 12

1½ cups flour
  2 teaspoons baking powder
  ½ teaspoon salt
  ½ teaspoon cinnamon
  ½ cup sugar
  ½ cup finely chopped dried apricots
  ½ cup finely chopped walnuts
  1 egg, slightly beaten
  1 cup milk
  ¼ cup salad oil

Sift together flour, baking powder, salt, cinnamon, and sugar. Stir in apricots and walnuts; set aside. Combine remaining ingredients and add to dry mixture. Stir just until dry ingredients are moistened. Fill 12 greased 2¾-inch muffin cups *or* 42 greased 1½-inch muffin cups two-thirds full. Bake in a 425° oven 25 minutes for large muffins and 12 to 15 minutes for small muffins.

Poppy Seed Muffins

Makes approximately 12

  ¾ cup sugar
  ¼ cup butter *or* margarine, softened
  ½ teaspoon grated orange peel
  2 eggs
  2 cups flour
2½ teaspoons baking powder
  ½ teaspoon salt
  ¼ teaspoon ground nutmeg
  1 cup milk
  ½ cup golden raisins
  ½ cup chopped pecans
  ¼ cup poppy seeds

In a large mixing bowl cream sugar, butter, and orange peel until light and fluffy. Add eggs one at a time, beating well after each; set aside. Combine flour, baking powder, salt, and nutmeg. Alternately add flour mixture and milk to creamed mixture; blend well after each addition. Stir in raisins, nuts, and poppy seeds. Fill 12 greased 2¾-inch muffin cups three-fourths full. Bake in a 400° oven 20 minutes.

Banana Muffins

Makes 12

  2 cups flour
  ⅓ cup sugar
  2 teaspoons baking powder
1½ teaspoons cinnamon
  1 teaspoon salt
  1 cup milk
  1 cup mashed ripe bananas
  1 egg, beaten
  ¼ cup melted shortening
  1 tablespoon sugar
  ¼ teaspoon cinnamon

Sift together flour, sugar, baking powder, cinnamon, and salt; set aside. Combine milk, bananas, egg, and shortening; add to dry ingredients. Stir just until moistened. Fill 12 greased 2¾-inch muffin cups two-thirds full. Mix together remaining sugar and cinnamon; sprinkle on top of each muffin. Bake in 400° oven 25 minutes.

Chocolate Chip Muffins

Makes 12

  2 cups flour
  1 tablespoon baking powder
  1 teaspoon salt
  1 cup milk
  3 tablespoons melted butter
  1 egg, beaten
  1 teaspoon vanilla
  ½ cup light brown sugar
  1 6-ounce package miniature semisweet chocolate chips

Stir together flour, baking powder, and salt; set aside. Combine milk, butter, egg, vanilla, brown sugar, and chocolate chips. Add to dry ingredients. Stir just until moistened. Fill 12 greased 2¾-inch muffin cups two-thirds full. Bake in 425° oven 20 to 25 minutes.

Photo Opposite
Apricot Walnut Muffins

A Slice of Life

Edgar A. Guest

When the bees are in the clover,
And a blue sky's bending over
This old world aglow with sunshine
Just as far as I can see;
When the breezes are suggesting
All the happiness of resting
Though it's time to gather honey,
Then I'm glad I'm not a bee.

There are some who flit for money
As the bee goes after honey;
There are splendors all around them
Which they never pause to see.
They are slaves to Tyrant Duty,
But when summer spills her beauty
And makes days as fair as this one,
Then I'm glad I'm not a bee.

Oh! I think it is much better
Not to be a honey getter;
I would rather lie and dream here
Underneath this shady tree.
Let the busy bee keep working,
Here's a day just made for shirking;
In this lovely summer weather,
I don't want to be a bee.

Edgar A. Guest began his illustrious career in 1895 at the age of fourteen when his work appeared in the Detroit Free Press. *His column was syndicated in over 300 newspapers, and he became known as "The Poet of the People." Mr. Guest captured the hearts of vast radio audiences with his weekly program, "It Can Be Done" and, until his death in 1959, published many treasured volumes of poetry.*

John Slobodnik

Red Beans and Corn Bread

Wanda J. Wright

My favorite memories today are of the good country cooking I enjoyed as a child. One of the best meals I remember was the small, mottled brown beans known to those north of the Red River as pintos, but known to those of us in Texas as good old red beans.

The ability to cook red beans and corn bread was a prerequisite to marriage for Texas girls. We learned the culinary art as soon as we were tall enough to see over the cabinet top while standing on a footstool.

We could always count on having red beans and corn bread for dinner on washdays. Monday morning Mother would rise before the sun and get breakfast started. Then, like roosting chickens awakened by the first glow of sunrise, my two brothers and I would smell the bacon frying and crawl out of bed, wash the sleep from our eyes, and get ready for the day.

After a breakfast of bacon, eggs, grits, biscuits, and homemade jam, Mother sent us off to school. We knew the routine that would follow after we left.

Mother took out the heavy, cream-colored crockery pot from the pantry and scooped out several cups of dried beans. She sorted the beans into a heavy cast-iron dutch oven. After picking out the small rocks and clumps of dirt, straw, and warped beans from the batch, she rinsed them thoroughly by running water into the pot to cover the beans, draining it off, then repeating the process until she was satisfied that not one speck of dirt remained.

Then she covered the beans with a final pot of water and added salt, some salt pork for flavor, and one finely chopped clove of garlic. She placed the pot on the big kerosene stove and let the beans simmer throughout the day on the back burner.

At the end of the day, we came home from school and smelled the aroma of beans which permeated our small house. Mother would bring in the last of the clothes which had dried on the line out back. We folded them and put them away while she bathed and changed into a pretty, flowered dress.

My brothers and I would then sit at the table in the small kitchen and have oatmeal cookies and ice-cold milk while we did our homework. I still recall the warmth of that kitchen and the security that came from knowing I was loved.

After we finished our homework, we went outside to play. That's when Mother put on her apron and started the corn bread. It came out of the oven high and yellow with a lightly browned top. Mother cut it into squares and set it on the table with the bowl of hot, juicy red beans. Freshly churned butter and crisp green onions completed the meal.

Daddy sat at the head of the table and said, "Thank you, Lord," for the meal, and we started eating our hearty feast. We left the table full and happy.

I've had many fine meals since then, but none equal red beans and corn bread in a warm country kitchen.

Photo Opposite
THE AMPLE LARDER
Dick Dietrich

Country Morning

Grace Noll Crowell

I wakened to the cottonwood's bright,
    tinkling music box;
I heard the little meadow brook run
    barefoot on the rocks;
I took my wicker basket to the orchard,
    and I found

A thousand rubies where ripe plums lay
    sprinkled on the ground;
I heaped my basket high with them—
    I stole them from the bees;
I gathered frilly lettuce leaves and
    dew-wet garden peas;

A wind blew cool against my throat and
　　tangled in my hair;
The running shadows swept the grass;
　　the birds were everywhere,
And there were flowers down the land, and
　　tall ferns in the wood;

A world as lovely as it was when
　　God first called it good.
My garden was an Eden, and
　　my orchard sweet to see.
There was no fruiting tree at all
　　that was forbidden me.

Photo Overleaf
THE FARMER'S GARDEN
TREMPALEAU COUNTY, WISCONSIN
Tom Algire Photography

TRANQUIL WATERS
WESTERN NORTH CAROLINA
Frank J. Miller

Country CHRONICLE
— Lansing Christman —

Oh, to be young again now that June has blossomed and fills the world with life; to be barefoot and carefree, romping on the carpet of lush, green grass of the lawn and splashing in the cold creek.

As I lie here in my hammock, I remember another, smaller hammock tied between two smaller trees. As a child, I spent hours reading and dreaming under those trees, while young birds chirped from their nest above me. Too curious to be sensible, I climbed the bending branches of the elm many times to see the scraggly baby orioles. For days I watched

the mother bring them bugs and worms to eat until they learned to fly and left me to my books.

Let me be young again, reading or swinging in the hammock, or playing in the woods near our house. A spring-fed creek ran along the wood's edge to a small, still pond fringed with ferns and marsh marigolds. The sun warmed the cold water so I could dangle my exposed feet from the rock where I sat. Each time I moved, tadpoles scattered away from my shadow.

In the pasture around the pond I entertained my

REDWOOD GROVE
NORTHERN CALIFORNIA
Gene Ahrens

mind by lying flat on my back and watching the clouds gracefully float across the blue ocean of sky above me. When I had imagined the clouds as every shape I could think of and I was sleepy from the warm sun, I jumped up and raced with the wind to the old stone wall that encircled the pasture. At six years old, I could just look over at the meadow on the other side. The shade beneath the wall was refreshing, and I drew shapes in the cool earth with a stick as moss and sheep sorrel kept watch there.

Yes, June has brought new life back to this earth. And time has brought some changes. That barefoot boy has grown, and his dreams and fantasies are tucked far away in a corner of his mind. They are waiting for days like today, when memories of a long-ago June conjure up a world of distant horizons, towering hilltops, and the miracle of new life. Today my once-distant horizons seem so near at hand, and once-towering hills are little more than gentle slopes now that they have been scaled and their vistas studied.

Oh, to be young once again, full of wonder at the world, swaying in a hammock under the boughs of great trees now that summer caresses the land.

The author of two published books, Lansing Christman has been contributing to Ideals *for almost twenty years. Mr. Christman has also been published in several American, foreign, and braille anthologies. He and his wife, Lucile, live in rural South Carolina where they enjoy the pleasures of the land around them.*

Old-Fashioned Things

Edna Jaques

The grace of plain old-fashioned things:
    An iron skillet piping hot,
An apple tree with spreading limbs,
    A bed of blue forget-me-nots.

The faded blue of overalls,
    Blue granite pans of wrinkled cream,
A backwoods farm where a kind old man
    Still does his plowing with a team.

Steep hills that seem to rise and rise
    Until they touch the sky's blue dome;
An old cow roundly strolling down
    Across the pasture fields for home.

A pile of wood cut up and split,
    Drying and curing in the sun,
A cobbler's bench in an old, worn shed
    Where any odd bit of work is done.

A farmhouse kitchen warm and clean
    That has a special kind of smell
Of homemade bread and pies and meat,
    Where plain God-fearing people dwell.

They miss so much who never know
    The joy that country living brings—
Star-studded nights and rosy dawns,
    The grace of plain old-fashioned things.

Photo Opposite
TEAMWORK
CHESTER, NEW HAMPSHIRE
Bill Hebden

THROUGH MY WINDOW

Pamela Kennedy

The sun streaks the sky above the misty mountains with reds and oranges, and the doves and cardinals begin their early conversations. In the harbor small boats and tugs commence their morning chores, hauling, pushing, scurrying about the Navy's business. It is morning in Pearl Harbor, and out my window I see the waterfront awaken. Soon the sounds of engines and ships, splashing wakes, and tooting whistles will drown out the birds, and the day's business will be underway.

But now, when things are still just shaking off the night's cool grasp, I walk across the dew-damp grass to stand behind the white curve of the Arizona Memorial and watch the sun come up.

We live on tiny Ford Island in the middle of the harbor and have a private view of this most public spectacle. It is a monument I have come to love, not only for what it brings to mind of past events, but for what it says to me of America now and in the future; for the Memorial represents to me what is the very best about my country.

The slender, white saddle of concrete sits astride a sunken battleship; its twenty-one open windows a silent salute to the fallen ones whose names are engraved upon its marble walls.

Each day thousands of visitors take the five-minute boat ride out to stroll the breezy corridor and gaze into the water below. Some remember vividly, others vaguely recall, but many are too young to have a memory of December 7, 1941. They come to try to understand something of what our country was and what it is to be.

The monument, built upon the wreckage of a war, reflects simplicity and strength, confirming to all who visit that America is a land where men can triumph over wrong. The only outside adornment is an abstract tree of life created of stained glass. A mute reminder, it affirms that those who gave themselves for freedom's cause will live on in the future of the country they served so well. Spanning the sunken Arizona's hull, the monument is actually a bridge which takes the mind from past to present, from despair to hope, from defeat to victory. And perhaps it is this aspect of the shrine which draws me most, for I am an optimist. I see the hopes and dreams of America still bright in the people of our land. They are building upon the failures of the past, constructing bridges of hope and expectation, living in a land secured by priceless sacrifices of those who lived before.

Today, when Navy ships glide past the Arizona Memorial, their crews still man the rails and render honors to their sister ship. Young men who only know of World War II from history books and movies salute with pride. In solemn rows they observe with clarity the heavy cost of freedom, and patriotism becomes reality once more.

It is so easy now to cast a cynical eye upon our nation, to complain about her weaknesses and wail about her woes. That's why I come here in the morning light to see in simple lines and clear-cut angles a symbol of her strength. At 8:00 A.M. the bugler sounds the call and the American flag is raised above the Arizona. "The Star-Spangled Banner" drifts across the harbor on the morning breeze, and my heart swells again with pride. Here, in the middle of the world's greatest ocean, the words seem true. America is still the land of the free and, with God's help, she will continue to be the home of the brave.

Pamela Kennedy is a freelance writer of short stories, articles, essays, and children's books. Married to a naval officer and mother of three children, she has made her home on both U.S. coasts and currently resides in Hawaii. She draws her material from her own experiences and memories, adding bits of imagination to create a story or mood.

THE REPUBLIC

Henry Wadsworth Longfellow

Thou, too, sail on, O Ship of State!
Sail on, O Union, strong and great!
Humanity with all its fears,
With all the hopes of future years,
Is hanging breathless on thy fate!
We know what Master laid thy keel,
What workmen wrought thy ribs of steel,
Who made each mast and sail and rope,
What anvils rang, what hammers beat,
In what a forge and what a heat
Were shaped the anchors of thy hope!
Fear not each sudden sound and shock;
'Tis of the wave and not the rock;
'Tis but the flapping of the sail
And not a rent made by the gale!
In spite of rock and tempest's roar,
In spite of false lights on the shore,
Sail on, nor fear to breast the sea!
Our hearts, our hopes, are all with thee,
Our hearts, our hopes, our prayers, our tears,
Our faith triumphant o'er our fears
Are all with thee—are all with thee!

USS ARIZONA MEMORIAL
PEARL HARBOR
OAHU, HAWAII
H. Armstrong Roberts, Inc.

50 YEARS AGO

Queen of England Captures America

Queen Elizabeth and Mrs. Roosevelt take in the sights of Washington as Washington takes in the Queen. The Queen has up her pearl-gray parasol. She wears gray crepe with a fox-edged jacket. Mrs. Roosevelt wears a tailored azure-blue wool dress presented by British sheep men. The small Queen's bright-blue eyes and quick curiosity charmed Washington.

As mysteriously and unpredictably as all such things happen, the King and Queen of England were a smash hit in the U.S. Through the first few days of their Canadian trip, some U.S. newspapers essayed a little mockery. The obvious irony of a British King's approach to an ex-British colony was news for some days. Then as they disappeared into the depths of the Canadian West, they almost dropped out of the news. When they re-emerged into it at Niagara Falls, everybody had begun to recognize the stubborn and modest industry of the King and the unquenchable vitality of his Queen. They had stood up without a falter under as exacting an ordeal as any traveling salesman has ever gone through; and they were gen-

38

uinely curious to know more and more about the Western Hemisphere.

But the sensation of the trip was the charm of the little Queen from Scotland. She had put aside the somewhat fussy clothes she wears in England and put on a superb collection by the British designer Hartnell. Her eyes looked astonishingly bright and blue, her figure slim, and nobody looked at the Queen with more interest than she looked back at them. The snob issue passed off without difficulty. American women did not curtsy and American men bowed as low as they wanted to or could. Good luck dogged the trip. The rain held off at the British Ambassador's garden party; and in the Washington parade, a tank that burst into flames was far back in the procession and hurt nobody.

King George VI places a wreath at the tomb of George Washington in Mount Vernon as Queen Elizabeth, Mrs. Roosevelt, Brig. Gen. E.M. Watson, and President Roosevelt look on. Washington led the colonial revolt against the King's great-great-great-grandfather, George III, which led to American independence from British rule. The ceremony symbolized the long friendship between Great Britain and the United States. Later the King praised American spirit and the diversity of races, creeds, and political beliefs in American society.

Said *The Times* of London last week, delighted by its sovereigns' success: "The event must hold the imagination of anyone with a feeling for history— King George VI entering as an honored guest, with floodlights and music and cheering, the great territory from which the last representatives of King George III withdrew in bitterness and defeat more than a century and a half ago. . . . No political motive prompted the visit."

President Roosevelt's sentiment when he toasted the king at the White House State dinner was: "It is because each nation is lacking in fear of the other that we have unfortified borders between us."

Remembering Dad

Lazy days near the little stream,
Winter storms of snowmen and sledding;
These things seem
To remind me of Dad.

Walking on the beach along the bay,
Drowsy drives on the mountain road;
These things seem to say
Remember Dad.

Tinsel and toy soldiers on a Christmas tree,
Easter baskets and bunnies;
I can still see
Dad.

Betty J. Silconas
Sparta, New Jersey

For My Dad

For the years of work and sacrifice
   You've gone through on my behalf,
For the special family times we had
   When we would have fun and laugh,
For instilling in me firm principles
   Of what's good and right and true,
And for making me aware to be
   Responsible in all I do,
For loving me when I was good,
   Still loving me when I was bad,
For never neglecting your duties
   As a faithful, loyal Dad,
For always sticking in there
   When the times were hard and rough,
For giving up your wants and dreams
   When there wasn't money enough,
And now as we grow older,
   For the special times we share,
When we say or do some special thing
   To show how much we care;
For all these things and many more,
   My heart just wants to say
I'm so proud you are my father
   And I love you more each day.

Deborah Derr Ellenberger
Harrisburg, Pennsylvania

Reflections

Portrait of a Father

A little child looks up to him;
He always says, "It's no bother
To mend a broken toy or two."
That's a portrait of a father.

He's always there for a good-night kiss or
"May I have a glass of water?"
He's always there when they need him most;
That's a portrait of a father.

He helps them learn to tie their shoes,
Fix a scarf, or straighten a collar.
He helps to feed them when they're young;
That's a portrait of a father.

There are clothes and food, dances and sports;
He'd give them his last dollar.
He teaches respect and dignity;
That's a portrait of a father.

Love surrounds this portrait made of
God's masterpiece of man.
Picture perfect he won't always be;
But that too is part of God's plan.

Ellen Rose
Springfield, Ohio

Editor's Note: Readers are invited to submit unpublished, original poetry, short anecdotes, and humorous reflections on life for possible publication in future *Ideals* issues. Please send copies only; manuscripts will not be returned. Writers receive $10 for each published submission. Send material to "Readers' Reflections," Ideals Publishing Corporation, P.O. Box 140300, Nashville, Tennessee 37214-0300.

A Carnation for You

A carnation for your buttonhole
On Father's Day, my dear,
When the children have all grown,
We'll celebrate with cheer.
An understanding husband,
A most dear and loving Dad,
You are the very best
A lucky family ever has had.

Hilda M. Krohn
Accord, New York

Earthbound Mockingbirds

Fleur K. D'Eramo

It was the Fourth of July. Traditionally even the most retiring person turns extrovert on Independence Day. It's as American as apple pie to be heard on the Fourth of July, whether shouting for recognition at the family picnic, screaming at the umpire at the ball park, or just marveling at the colorful explosions of a fireworks display; and everything on the Fourth begins with a parade of brass and drums.

But my husband and I were in a *Walden* mood, feeling an inner joy of contentment in our status quo, and we wanted to pay tribute to our Founding Fathers in our own way. So we made our escape from Cleveland, that bustling jumble of shipping, yachting, and trade which clings to the edge of Lake Erie.

Our search for quiet and tranquillity took us south to that part of Ohio where the land breathes the sweet, tree-filtered air, and small towns display white church steeples instead of skyscrapers; where county roads lead to no place in particular, and rural mailboxes are still mounted on fence posts with morning glories smiling skyward.

When we picked up our southbound road and left the city behind us, we felt like birds looking for a territory stake, having all the great green spaces from which to choose! We maneuvered east to Wooster (Tree City, USA), where the traditional Fourth was in full swing with the usually quiet community playing host. Visitors were sampling clean air and country music and generally going native all over the wide streets which were quite unaccustomed to such an assault of conviviality. Large signs promised a pyrotechnical display after sundown, and hawkers were setting up refreshment stands on the college campus.

We drove south to Millersburg and even that "end of the world" retreat was roaring with people. We followed a one-track lane east to a place where a stand of poplar braved the July heat, and a grove of black locust offered filtered light and cooling shade. We had arrived! Our stake spread out before us, and we proceeded to lay claim to it with music racks, two rosewood recorders (one alto and one soprano) made for us in the Black Forest, and a stack of music with clothespins as insurance against the breeze.

We felt like privileged people indeed, for we had encountered no other human being. Ralph Waldo Emerson wrote, "In the woods we return to reason and faith." And the healing balm was so real as to be tangible. Birds chorused; each one singing his own theme song, yet somehow blending into symphony. Small mammals scurried from cover to cover, and the heat of the sun shimmered the air above the grass.

We tuned up and began with Mozart for sheer perfection and delight; then on to Corelli, Vivaldi, and Bach. Recorders are peculiarly right in the open air; their rounded tones are embraced by the atmosphere; they do not pierce the void but are softly cradled by it.

We played on and on, feeling separated from reality and transported by the inspiration of the Masters. When at last we stopped, it seemed that the woodland was holding its breath. Then out of the shadows stepped a man with his dog. He said, "Are you aware that all the birds stopped singing the moment you began to play? Listen! They're still silent, waiting for your concert to continue."

As we talked to the man and made friends with his dog, the birds gradually resumed their own chorusing. The spell was broken and the rafters rang with what must have been post-concert small talk in the lobby of Ohio's open-air concert hall.

It has been said that many symphonic themes were first suggested to the composers as they listened to the original music makers—the birds in the trees. If these same birds fell silent in order to listen to man's efforts with instruments and scores, did they recognize flashbacks of melody once their own? Did they marvel at these new earthbound mockingbirds paying tribute in their own way to the Founding Fathers on the Fourth of July?

Pototschnik.

When We Build

John Ruskin

When we build, let us think that we build
forever. Let it not be for present delight
nor for present use alone. Let it be such work
as our descendants will thank us for, and let us
think, as we lay stone on stone, that a time is to
come when those stones will be held sacred because
our hands have touched them, and that men will say
as they look upon the labor and wrought substance
of them,

   "See! This our Fathers did for us."

Blinker

John Moring

A sound in silence
Green upon green
Motionless
It blinks once and stretches a webbed foot.
Startled by passing footsteps,
The blinker springs into the wetness.
The green is empty—
Save for a ripple on the water.
But soon he is back,
Settled and motionless,
Sighing for a moment.
Curious of a passing fly,
The blinker almost smiles
But lets the insect pass.
Better fare will enter the green—
One only has to wait.
Motionless
Silent
It blinks again.

The Cricket

Frederick Goddard Tuckerman

The humming bee purrs softly o'er his flower;
    From lawn and thicket
The dog-day locust singeth in the sun
    From hour to hour:
Each has his bard, and thou, ere day be done,
    Shalt have no wrong.
So bright that murmur mid the insect crowd,
Muffled and lost in bottom-grass, or loud
    By pale and picket:
Shall I not take to help me in my song
    A little, cooing cricket?

46

Strange Traveler

Maurine Martin

Look! There beside that brownish rock.
It moved! I know it did!
It looks just like another rock,
But it moved a bit and slid.

Look now—A nose is poking out
And two small searching eyes. . . .
It looks as though it's wondering
If moving would be wise.

To move, his house must go along.
It's fastened to his back.
So naturally, it slows him down
On smooth or stony track.

But how good to have a shelter
To keep him nice and dry,
And a roof to give him shade
From the summer sun on high.

Perhaps he's traveling down this path
To join his friends and kin. . . .
So travel on. I'll stand aside,
Mr. Terrapin!

47

What Makes a Nation Great?

Alexander Blackburn

Not serried ranks with flags unfurled,
Not armored ships that gird the world,
Not hoarded wealth nor busy mills,
Not cattle on a thousand hills,
Not sages wise, nor schools nor laws,
Not boasted deeds in freedom's cause—
All these may be, and yet the state
In the eye of God be far from great.

That land is great which knows the Lord,
Whose songs are guided by His word;
Where justice rules 'twixt man and man,
Where love controls in art and plan;
Where, breathing in his native air,
Each soul finds joy in praise and prayer—
Thus may our country, good and great,
Be God's delight—man's best estate.

From *THE WORLD'S BEST-LOVED POEMS* edited by James
Gilchrist Lawson. Copyright 1927 by Harper & Row,
Publishers, Inc., renewed 1955 by Camilla Martens Lawson.
Reprinted by permission of Harper & Row, Publishers, Inc.

Photo Opposite
COLORADO RIVER
TOROWEAP POINT, NORTH RIM
GRAND CANYON, ARIZONA
Ed Cooper Photography

Bare Feet

Esther Kem Thomas

When the garden's made, and the fields
    sprout corn,
And the blackbirds caw, high and forlorn;
When Grandma brews her sassafras,
And the air is fresh with new-cut grass
It's the time of year no joys compete
With the feel of the ground to a kid's
    bare feet!

My, those digits spread like a human fan
In the prickly grass, but a sharp rock can
Scrouge 'em up to a fluted cup

Till the tender sort of toughens up
In a day or two; what a yearly treat
Is the feel of the ground to a kid's
    bare feet!

How innocent the grassy lawn
To hide so much to step upon,
But a summer's end finds a sole
    and heel
Immune to rock or bark or steel!
No path of roses man has trod
In luxury, and leather-shod
For satisfaction, reigns complete
Like the feel of the ground to a kid's
    bare feet!

To Cap It!

Helen Harrington

All winter long I fought the fight
To have them put their caps on right—
The woolly ones with furry flaps,
But they would not wear their caps!

I found them on the icy pond
Or on the ski slope just beyond,
Or with their skates, or on their sleds—
Anywhere but on their heads!

But now that the baseball season's on
Can't you guess what they want to don?

Their baseball caps! The striped ones!
It seems they couldn't get home runs
Without those caps! Sometimes it's like
They couldn't even get a strike!

They wear them backwards and awry,
Pushed or pulled across one eye!
Hanging barely by an ear,
Stoically, or with a sneer!

To the park, to school, and on the street!
They wear them even when they eat!
Without a baseball cap to wear,
A boy just seems completely bare!

Child's Play

Monday's Child

Monday's child is fair of face,

Tuesday's child is full of grace,

Wednesday's child is full of woe,

Thursday's child has far to go.

Friday's child is loving, giving,

Saturday's child works hard for a living,

And a child that is born on the Sabbath day
Is fair and wise and good and gay.

Pheasant in the Grass

Grace Noll Crowell

A startled brilliance in the wayside grass
Quiets to let me pass,
And loath to miss that gorgeous hidden thing,
I pause . . . a scintillating wing,
A scuttling tail of flame glides through the weeds,
Scattering the ripening seeds,
And through the thinning stems I see him there:
A glory on the air,
A bright metallic sheen of colored light,
Blinding my sight;
Scarlet and purple, crimson, gold, and blue—
The wire grasses part to let him through:
That crested knight, that splendor-feathered king.
And I am left, remembering
An unforgettable thing:
My mind still spangled with beauty past and done
As eyes light from looking at the sun.

A Bird Came down the Walk

Emily Dickinson

A Bird came down the Walk—
He did not know I saw—
He bit an Angleworm in halves
And ate the fellow, raw,

And then he drank a Dew
From a convenient Grass—
And then hopped sidewise to the Wall
To let a Beetle pass—

He glanced with rapid eyes
That hurried all around—
They looked like frightened Beads, I thought—
He stirred his Velvet Head

Like one in danger, Cautious,
I offered him a Crumb
And he unrolled his feathers
And rowed him softer home—

Than Oars divide the Ocean,
Too silver for a seam—
Or Butterflies, off Banks of Noon
Leap, plashless as they swim.

© John Sl...

Tomfoolery

Gail R. Wyatt

There he sits. He is concentrating very hard on catching a particularly "buzzy" fly that is circling his head. That's it, Tom Cat! Follow him to the window! Against the bright daylight the fly is defined sharply—at least to me. But Tom Cat is nearly blind, so it is the sound of the buzzing which will help him zero in and trap his prey.

Quietly listening, moving not a muscle except for his sleek, black tail, he waits. That tail moves like a snake ready to strike, but the fly does not see that. He only sees what must appear to be a black and white statue of a cat, sitting near the window. Suddenly my old friend lifts one paw, and then another, and I do not hear that particularly "buzzy" fly anymore.

We bought Tom Cat for a quarter from two little boys who were not at all sure they wanted to part with any of the five kittens their mother cat had surprised them with. My own little boys were amazed to discover that one can of cat food cost more than their whole cat did! We chose Tom Cat over the other kittens because of his big eyes: he had the prettiest big, green cat eyes we had ever seen. How could we have known then that he could not see very well with those lovely eyes?

We began to suspect that there was something peculiar about Tom Cat when he fell down the basement steps—a very un-cat-like thing to do. We noticed that he could span the distance between the reclining chair and the sofa—almost! He could jump up on the windowsill—almost! Perhaps, we thought, we should have named him Tomfoolery Cat instead of just plain Tom Cat. Yet we could call him from our front door, and he would scamper down the towering maple tree, across the neighbor's lawn, over the rosebush, up the steps, and into the house, a darting patch of black and white. He never missed! That is, until one day when one of our boys set a rather large bag of groceries down on the front porch. We called Tom Cat, and he scampered down the towering maple tree, across the neighbor's lawn, over the rosebush, up the steps, and smack into the bag of groceries! He sat there rather stunned. We were rather stunned too. He appeared to be slightly embarrassed and not at all pleased that we had finally discovered his secret. Tom Cat had mapped out all his favorite places in his mind. But if anything were moved, even slightly, he ran right into it.

As I watch him navigate the living room, brushing against objects and deciding which way to go, I wonder if he minds being different. He plays and romps like any other cat (maybe more like a kitten). He listens much better than any child! No, he doesn't seem to mind not seeing as well as other cats. We don't mind either.

Artwork Opposite
COZY NAPTIME
Original Painting by John Sloan

The Farm

Alice B. Dorland

Among your childhood memories
Is there a farm?
And on this farm a wondrous barn,
Sweet, vast, and dusty dim,
With pigeons murmuring in the lofty cupola
And moted sunlight filtering through the chinks?

Our childhood barn had hand-hewn beams
Festooned with wisps of hay,
And in their corners spiders spun their webs.
Remember how we children walked those beams
And dared each other jump from this high one or that
To fragrant slippery hay below,
And how we slid down to the floor
Where kittens were at play?

Remember the old shepherd dog
That helped round up the cows each day,
And how they marched into the barn,
Each to her accustomed stall?

I still hear the soft, padded sound
Their hooves made on the wooden floor,
Their tossing heads and swishing tails,
The sound of milk hitting the pails.
Remember its sweet smell.

Remember how old Rover
Churned the butter every week?
I still can see him in the wooden treadmill,
Still hear its clatter and its creak.

Remember how we watched the hired man
Chop off the chickens' heads
Out by the barn
Each Saturday and Wednesday morn?

Remember, too, the ice-cream churn,
Its wheel we were allowed to turn
Till little arms grew tired?
I close my eyes and taste again
The sweet vanilla cream
That clung to the cold dasher.

Remember the young calves at play
That let us pat their heads
And rub the knobby little bumps
That would be horns some day?
Remember their inquiring eyes,
Their rough, pink tongues,
Their soft, brown fur?

The kindly, stalwart horses, too,
Were our good friends.
I feel, again, old Prince's velvet lips
As he took apples from my little palm.

The Colt

Alexandra Gabriel

You can tell he is born to be noble:
He has such a solemn gaze.
Witness his dignified silence
As he passes these grassy June days.

They keep their own counsel, these horses,
And say nothing about the warm sun
Or the cool creek to which they lower their lips
Or the earth under hoof as they run.

So of course the colt never babbles
About changes in the weather
Or interrupts moments of music
He discerns among fellows of feather.

I hope he will take me riding one day.
If I too am silent, I'll see
How little of horse ever touches the ground,
So fine-footed and regal is he.

Photo Opposite
FRESH INSPIRATION
L. Willinger
FPG International

How Does She Do It?

Linda M. Massen

One thing about us kids, when Mom speaks, we listen.

"Supper!" Mom's voice booms through the clapboard walls of the old farmhouse. Bodies drop out of trees. The shed door squeaks open. A hoe rattles against the railing spindles. My brothers and sisters force their bikes over the country gravel to get home in time for supper. Mom only says it once. Matter of fact, Mom says most things just once. We either hear her, or we don't. If we aren't there on time . . . well, the fried chicken and mashed potatoes do a disappearing act faster than a hare in a dog pen. I still remember spending one long night with an empty feeling in my stomach. I napped on the davenport that afternoon and didn't hear Mom's call. There is always a heap of food so long as your ears are spry and your eyes open, especially during the day when they're supposed to be.

You should see Mom whip out pies. On bone-growin' days, that's what Mom calls them, I pass through the kitchen about every ten minutes just to keep an eye on things, you understand. Sometimes I catch her with one of those crusts a-swinging elbow high and lots of little dough scraps just about bite-sized winking on the table. Every one of those tiny pieces is staring right in my direction cryin', "Eat me! Eat me!" which, of course, I do when Mom turns to lay the pastry in the tin. Before you know it, bing! bing! bing! six apple pies are steaming on the table and not a crumb in sight, thanks to yours truly.

Talkin' about heaps of things, the laundry in a big family has to be about the largest man-made formation in the world. Mom gets up early—earlier than us kids. It's before first light. I know that 'cause I hear her feeling her hand down the hall wall outside our room on the way to the bathroom. It's dark, and I'm scared of the dark; so usually I stick my face into the bed and hide under the pillow till I hear everyone bickerin'. Most days, Mom's wringing and hanging laundry out to dry all day between other chores. We kids help, but she's the one who really gets things done. She stretches the clothes on the outside line all times of the year. Round about the first frost, when the pumpkins come in, we are likely to find our shirts frozen solid on the line; but we just hang 'em around the kitchen to thaw, and Buddy, the inside mutt, laps up the puddles under our cuffs and tails. Sometimes in the winter Mom just takes it into her head to hang out the long johns. No reflection on us kids, you understand. It's a sight from a scare show, all those long red and white woolly things clacking full of icicles. Mom claims it's healthy, though, and none of us ever gets too sick, so I guess there's something to it.

We pretty much live off the land here in Ohio. Every one of us kids pitches in, although it's not from the goodness of our hearts. Our family garden plot is about the biggest blister factory in this section of the country, especially around August when the weeds take vitamins and the rains take vacations. Mom works out there every day pulling intruders in her plantings. She hoes and harvests and then puts up the food for winter. Mom never cries or complains like the rest of us. Maybe she just doesn't have time to think about it.

Yes, Mom sure is a strong person. She lets us younguns do something wrong once, but we better not repeat the same mistake. Course, with each of us sixteen kids doing a certain type of mischief once (once apiece, that is, and every kid gettin' a fair shot at bein' bad), well, it makes life lively when we're all in the same bean row tryin' to look busy. You want to know how she does it, I mean hold us porch hounds to one time each for every rotten thing we can think up?

Well, I was six years old when she sat me down with the rest of the middle-sized bunch. They were plucking chickens for supper. She showed me how to do the easy parts and passed me on to my sister. Now, plucking chickens is downright unappealing to a six-year-old. Sis slapped that ol' worn-out layin' hen on the board in front of me and I squirmed; I set my lips together and stared at that thing, but I never did touch it. That night at dinner when the whole family was together, an iron hand held back my wrist as I picked a drumstick off the pile. Can you believe I picked it up, felt the crispy crumbs, smelled the fat sizzlin', and Mom stopped me from havin' it?

"Hold on there, little one. You didn't share in the fixin' of that chicken, and you ain't gonna share in the eatin' of it." The potatoes were pretty good, but I longed for that leg. I learned a lot about Mom that night. Even when she's not there, she's there; she knows. She sure knew about me and that chicken. And the next day I made sure she saw me pulling those little pin feathers with all my might. Once, that's all it takes with Mom.

Actually, Mom's soft on the babies. She cleaves to them like a hen to her eggs. Nothin' she likes better than a baby waddlin' around making goo-goo noises. She cuddles 'em and croons to 'em till their faces crack into smiles. But there isn't any syrup in her ways. No, Mom's just one of those strong, calm people whose deep-down voice can turn a baby's head.

Mom doesn't expect us to be perfect or smart or anything special. She just takes each one of us as we come. There's no molding of children. But each of us knows right from wrong, and we take our licks for what we know is right. Mom makes sure of that. She takes care of us and she keeps us in line. "What you take is what you eat," Mom gently reminds us from time to time when we forget to sop the gravy with our bread. But we're so hungry most days, our plates gleam like they were washed already. We kids jostle up real close on the wide, old farmstead. And we keep an ear open and our eyes sharp to learnin' to be keen, quick, and mannerly. Yep, in this family it certainly is true that when Mom talks, we kids listen. And that's how she keeps us all in line.

Ebb Tide

Agnes Davenport Bond

My ship of dreams is out on the sea,
And the waves are flying high.
The ocean winds are sharp and free
As they pierce the western sky.

The tide is out and the shore is bare
Far up on the sandy beach;
But the racing billows leap and tear
At the strand beyond their reach.

The sea gulls circle just overhead,
While they peer about in quest,
Then quickly drop with wings outspread
And ride on the foaming crest.

A fisherman's craft is bobbing about
A mile or farther away,
But my gaze is lingering farther out
Where my dream ship cruised today.

It still is sailing far out on the sea,
It is nearly beyond my ken.
I wonder if it will come back to me
When the tide comes in again.

Photo Opposite
PEMAQUID LIGHTHOUSE
PEMAQUID, MAINE
Laatsch-Hupp Photo

BITS &

What constitutes the bulwark of our own liberty and independence? It is not our frowning battlements or bristling seacoasts, our army and navy. These are not our reliance against tyranny. All of those may be turned against us without making us weaker for the struggle. Our reliance is in the love of liberty which God has planted in us. Our defense is in the spirit which prized liberty as the heritage of all men in all lands everywhere. Destroy this spirit and you have planted the seeds of despotism at your own doors.

Abraham Lincoln

God made the country, and man made the town. What wonder, then, that health and virtue should most abound and least be threatened in the fields and groves.

William Cowper

With malice toward none; with charity for all; with firmness in the right, as God gives us to see the right, let us strive on to finish the work we are in; to bind up the nation's wounds; to care for him who shall have borne the battle, and for his widow, and his orphan—to do all which may achieve and cherish a just and lasting peace among ourselves and with all nations.

Abraham Lincoln

The country is both the philosopher's garden and his library, in which he reads and contemplates the power, wisdom, and goodness of God.

William Penn

PIECES

The men who won in the Revolution and made this country take its place among the nations of the earth did it because they had in them courage, resolution, integrity, unbending will, and common sense.

Theodore Roosevelt

Remember that there is an atheism which still repeats the creed. There is a belief in God which does not bring Him; nay, rather say, which does not let Him come into close contact with our daily life. The very reverence with which we honor God may make us shut Him out of the hard tasks and puzzling problems with which we have to do. Many of us who call ourselves theists are like the savages who, in the desire to honor the wonderful sundial which had been given them, built a roof over it. Break down the roof; let God in on your life.

Phillips Brooks

The truest test of civilization is not the census, not the size of cities, nor the crops; no, but the kind of man the country turns out.

Ralph Waldo Emerson

Greatness is a spritual condition worthy to excite love, interest, and admiration; and the outward proof of professing greatness is that we excite love, interest, and admiration.

Matthew Arnold

If you would be known and not know, vegetate in a village. If you would know and not be known, live in a city.

Caleb Colton

A Noiseless, Patient Spider

Walt Whitman

A noiseless, patient spider,
I mark'd, where, on a little promontory, it
    stood, isolated;
Mark'd how, to explore the vacant, vast
    surrounding,
It launch'd forth filament, filament,
    filament, out of itself;
Ever unreeling them—ever tirelessly speeding
    them.

And you, O my Soul, where you stand
Surrounded, surrounded, in measureless
    oceans of space,
Ceaselessly musing, venturing, throwing—
    seeking the spheres, to connect them,
Till the bridge you will need be form'd—till
    the ductile anchor hold;
Till the gossamer thread you fling catch
    somewhere, O my Soul.

Photo Opposite
GARDEN SPIDER AT HOME
RIVERFIELD WILDLIFE SANCTUARY
LOUISVILLE, KENTUCKY
Adam Jones

My Birthday

Ray Koonce

Increasingly my prayer has become, "Lord, teach me to delight in simple things and help me to simplify my life so as to make room for them." My seventy-fifth birthday is looking me squarely in the face. It has suddenly dawned upon me that old age can be the most unexpected of all things that can happen to a person. Being older does undeniably bring its disadvantages, but when all of my limitations have been acknowledged, some genuine compensations which old age brings are apparent. I intend to fully enjoy and make the most of these days, leaving the future in the hands of God, knowing, as the Psalmist declared, "My times are in thy hand."

The greatest blessing of these years is the time I have to enjoy some of life's benefits which were formerly overlooked or for which there was insufficient time. These years are giving me time to enjoy friends in a more leisurely way. It's nice to be able to say to those who drop by, "Oh, do sit down and visit. No, I'm *not* in a hurry." It's nice, too, to be able to sit rocking on my front porch and say to friends passing by, "Come and sit awhile. Let's talk." I'm realizing that the chief ornament of our home at any time is the friend or friends visiting. I'm delighted

A pilot told me of an experience when he was flying a plane crowded with passengers. A sudden storm struck just as they passed the dangerous peaks of the Rocky Mountains, and for a few terrible minutes he had not been sure they would make it. Then with one final flash of lightning and a crash of thunder, the storm broke away and they emerged into a tremulous sunlight. Then, keeping pace with them as they flew was that lovely symbol, the pilot's cross—the shadow of the plane on the clouds. Flung around it was a halo of light, and beyond that, a rainbow. "For a single instant," he said, "I saw the beauty and the perfection of the world, and I felt as if I were one with it."

It is moments like these in which we truly live, and I'm discovering more of them as I grow older. These moments come as one stands and watches the summer storm as the thunder crashes, the lightning rips the sky, the branches of the trees bend, bow, and sweep the ground as the powerful winds rake them. It is in moments like these that we truly live and a kind of glory lights our minds as we sense the magnificence of the universe and the Power which lies behind it.

When I was asked recently if I told my age, my reply was, "Of course. I don't mind *telling* my age. I just mind *being* my age." But why should I resent becoming seventy-five years old this birthday? I don't, for I have come to see that as we grow older, we can enjoy even richer, fuller, and more satisfying lives.

to have the time these days to enjoy the glory of friendship and to know the spiritual inspiration which comes when one discovers that someone else trusts and believes in him.

An additional benefit of these later years is the privilege of having time to thoroughly enjoy and appreciate my family, including our grandchildren. Family jokes are part of the cement which keeps our family close, and we share a lot of "remember whens?" at family gatherings. We enjoy being together just for the sake of being together. Our children have become our best friends. These days have also given Virginia, my wife, and me more time to be together and to enjoy each other. Virginia has always been a wise wife who knew when to overlook and when to oversee. She has found it necessary to do much more overlooking than overseeing since my retirement has supplied her with more husband than she has grown accustomed to.

These golden years are bringing unprecedented leisure time for all of the activities which were formerly crowded out by the pressures of work and responsibility: reading, writing, travel, yard work, rocking on our front porch, and meditating about the meaning and wonder of life. This opportunity has brought home the truth of Emerson's discovery that being alive is sometimes an almost unbearable pleasure. In the rush of living, our senses grow dull and cease to feel the ecstasy of life. Some of our best moments are dulled by our cares and anxieties. It is helpful to remember that every moment is a glorious gift from God, and there is significance in everything if we look for it.

COLLECTOR'S CORNER

Zithers

Bashful Brother Oswald's blue banjo

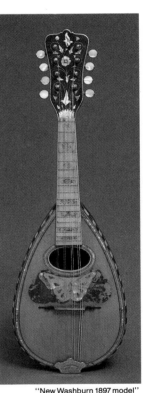

"New Washburn 1897 model"
bowl back mandolin

Roy Acuff's name is synonymous with the Grand Ole Opry and with country music in general. His long and distinguished career as singer, fiddler, and songwriter has earned him the title of "The King of Country Music." While traveling around the country, Mr. Acuff (a born collector who started out collecting guns, hand-painted neckties, and ancient record players) accumulated a wide variety of handsome and unusual musical instruments because, in his words, each "had a story." Collecting musical instruments is indeed like collecting stories. An instrument is like a seed, ready at any time to burst into bloom. When you hold an old mandolin in your hands, you have only to close your eyes to imagine the pleasure and comfort its gentle sounds have produced over the years.

America's history sparkles with music played at square dances, county fairs, and down-home get-togethers where people assembled from miles around to trade instruments, swap tunes, and share their ethnic musical backgrounds. As America's musical tradi-

tions developed, instrument makers, both professional and amateur, adapted their designs from European prototypes. The dulcimer, for example, is a modified violin which is strummed, not bowed, and came into being when Appalachian church sects denounced the violin as "the devil's instrument." The autoharp, guitar, and mandolin owe their modern form to the zithers brought from eastern Europe.

Many collections begin with a fiddle, mandolin, or guitar inherited from grandparents whose own lives were blessed with the gift of music making. Attics yield long-silent instruments in need only of polish and new strings to be played once again or simply admired for the fine craftsmanship and ingenuity of their construction.

—from the Editor

Roy Acuff's Musical Collection

It is not surprising that Roy Acuff should have become so fascinated with stringed instruments as to build a museum around his collection. They have been a part of American culture since long before this diverse set of colonies became a nation. These instruments are portable, pleasant looking, provide accompaniment to the human voice and rhythm for dancing, and are all relatively easy for even the minimally gifted to coax a few tunes from with but a few hours of practice.

It is fitting that Roy Acuff should have chosen the fiddle as his instrument for it is the grandfather of all the stringed instruments in America. Originally refined to its present form in Italy around 1550, it quickly made its way all over Europe for it was small, light, easily carried, evocative in sound, and relatively easy to learn. That it was brought to the New World with the earliest settlers should be no surprise.

The banjo, too, has been a part of America's musical heritage for well over two centuries and, with the fiddle, was used for dances and get-togethers in colonial times. George Washington had a favorite tune—"Jaybird Sittin' on a Hickory Limb"—as did Thomas Jefferson in "Grey Eagle." Bashful Brother Oswald has played his famous "blue banjo" on countless stages with Roy Acuff over the course of the years. Actually, it is a medium-priced banjo of the mid-1930s.

The zither is a folk instrument of northern European origin which can vary from a few strings to as many as forty or fifty or more. It is both fretted and plucked. Many zithers display meticulous craftsmanship in woodworking.

Many collectors favor bowl back mandolins which often show the lavish work of inlayers and designers. The mandolin became popular in America in the late 1880s. Elaborate ornamentation was the rule rather than the exception on these instruments, especially on higher quality bowl backs. After the 1920s, when the vogue for mandolin orchestras had come and gone, the instruments were turning up in music stores and hock shops at very cheap prices. It wasn't long, naturally, before the mandolin found its way into the hands of country musicians.

Roy has collected many instruments which belonged to well-known Opry performers whom Roy himself admires. Others reflect his passionate curiosity and interest in the many lands he has visited in his long career for Roy Acuff is an avid collector of the folk instruments of a wide variety and spectrum of cultures.

Roy states: "On all my trips around the world, I've gathered instruments and carried them in from all different parts of the globe and put them all on the wall for people to see, and I'm very proud of it. I've tried to make it interesting for people to look at."

Douglas B. Green and George Gruhn

Tamboritzas, Yugoslavian folk instruments

Roy Acuff's collection of fiddles, dulcimers, banjos, guitars, zithers, and other interesting stringed instruments, including a fine old harp! now resides at Opryland USA, Inc., Nashville, Tennessee.

73

FROM MY G·A·R·D·E·N JOURNAL

Deana Deck

The Delightful, Adaptable Daylily

To a lot of people, gardening just appears to be endless drudgery—digging, hoeing, raking, weeding, watering. This is frequently brought home to me when I'm asked to suggest things that can be grown without effort and to design a garden that can be planted and forgotten.

Of course, not everyone who asks about no-work gardening is anti-effort. Today many people just don't have the time. Raising a family, maintaining a household, and holding down a full-time career doesn't leave much time for gardening. And there are many dedicated, older gardeners who would love to spend every waking hour among the plants, armed with trowel and clippers and watering can but find they can no longer handle the physical effort that the annual or perennial bed demands.

For all who ask about truly maintenance-free gardening, for whatever reason, I have a handy, one-word solution: daylilies. Plant a few of these hardy little survivors and you'll have the best of all possible worlds: a garden that requires little or no work, plants that will spread and increase all by themselves, and a profusion of blooms to admire.

Daylilies, or *Hemerocallis*, are one of the oldest cultivated flowers. They originated in China and were known to the Greeks in early Christian times. The botanical name, in fact, is from the Greek words *hemero* (one day) and *callis* (beauty). The name is a little misleading however. It's true that each bloom

only lasts for a single day, but each scape, or flower-producing stem, can produce as many as fifty blooms over a period of several weeks. Their common name is misleading too. They are not lilies. They are fibrous-rooted herbaceous perennials.

Most people are familiar with the orange road-side daylily that blooms merrily away in the worst conditions imaginable. Daylilies are wondrously adaptive. They will grow in full sun or in shade, in hot climates or very cold ones, on mountainous terrain, flat prairies, or coastal hillsides. They grow equally well in damp, boggy areas and dry, well-drained locations. It's no wonder that when placed in a well-prepared flower bed they will thrive for years with no attention!

All varieties of daylily bulbs are planted in late March to early April in a ten- to twelve-inch deep bed. Add composted manure and a little bone meal before planting. The daylilies will bloom profusely without making any more demands on your time. It helps to dig them up and divide them every three or four years, but if you don't they will not suffer overmuch. The blooms may become smaller and fewer in number as the years progress, but this is easily reversed by dividing and replanting.

Hybridizers have created an abundance of bloom types, colors, and forms in recent years. One of their most delightful contributions to the species is a selection of early, mid-seasonal, and late blooming varieties. If you seek these out for planting you can have blooms all summer long. Another wonderful contribution of daylily breeders is the great profusion of colors that are now available. If you think daylilies have to be orange, think again. Today they are available in a wide range of colors and combinations that almost rival the iris. There are rich golds; deep, dark reds and wines; pale apricots and pinks; delicate whites; and vibrant magentas.

One reason that daylilies lend themselves so well to a low-maintenance garden is that they are nearly pest- and insect-free. They do suffer sometimes from spider mites in hot weather, but a good spraying with a strong stream of water will knock most mites off the plants. A word of caution here. Kelthane, which is widely used to eliminate spider mites from other plants, is harmful to the daylily. If you keep the plants healthy with an annual feeding of 5-10-5 fertilizer and hose them down periodically they will be able to withstand most mite infestations.

Daylily foliage will continue to remain green and healthy-looking long after other bulb foliage has begun to wither. For this reason, daylilies are an excellent addition to the bulb bed, where they can distract the eye from the unattractive fading foliage of tulips and narcissus. After each daylily has completed its blooming season, you should remove the flower stalks. These will dry out and begin to look like two-foot-tall sticks randomly stuck in your garden. Removing them is the simplest of garden tasks as they come loose quite easily.

In addition to their ease of care and the beauty they bring to the garden, daylilies have another virtue. Nearly every part of the plant is edible except the bulb itself. The bulbs of *all* lilies are considered poisonous. The buds, picked the day before opening, are delicious when added to salads or used in stir-fry dishes. Both buds and open blossoms can be added to salads or dipped in beaten egg, rolled in flour, and fried; and the young stalks can be cut just above the roots, cooked for a few minutes, and served with lemon and butter, just like asparagus!

Deana Deck's garden column is a regular feature in the Sunday Tennessean. *Ms. Deck is a frequent contributor to* Nashville *magazine and grows her daylilies in Nashville, Tennessee.*

Photo Overleaf
ANCIENT OAKS
OAK ALLEY PLANTATION
NEW ORLEANS, LOUISIANA
Bob Clemenz Photography

Country Dreaming

Loise Pinkerton Fritz

So oft I dream of the country.
In retrospect I see
The sun breaking through at dawning,
Opening the day like a key.

Oh, oft I dream of the country
When the sun shines bright at noon;
I see the strawberry blossoms
Turning to berries in June.

How oft I dream of the country!
On lovely moonlit nights,
I dream of country courting times,
Old-fashioned buggy rides.
Atop the hill, in silhouette,
The country church I see.
From each country scene I dream of
Stems a peaceful melody.

The Silent Songs

Mary Carlier

Of all my songs the silent ones are sweet:
A spider web quicksilvered in the mist,
The melody of sun and ripened wheat,
A bluebird's flight, a baby's trusting fist . . .

The lyric dream of daisies in the grass,
Bending and rising as my footsteps go;
The spice-wine scent of autumn days that pass
Into the pure white radiance of snow . . .

The pulse-notes in a butterfly's frail wing,
Wood embers glowing softly in the night,
The sudden joy that one dear friend can bring,
And eyes that meet mine over candlelight.

Great music comes; the quiet corners fill.
To me, the silent songs are sweeter still.

Readers' Forum

I have been receiving your magazine for about one year. It never fails to warm my heart and soul. I think everyone should read it and feel its joy. I look forward to every issue. Keep up the great work.

Judith A. Downey
Ponchatoula, Louisiana

I have enjoyed Ideals for several years. Last winter I moved to a housing for the elderly. After reading my Ideals each month, I have shared it with several friends here. Three of those have enjoyed it so much they have subscribed for their own. It is a beautiful magazine. Keep up the good work.

Mrs. Ellis L. Wilson
Wolfeboro, New Hampshire

I noticed several of your readers have written telling you what happens to their copies of Ideals. I thought you might be interested in what has happened to my copies over the years. I save them until September—then mail them to friends and relatives in Scotland, England, Germany, and Australia. I arrange to send each one a different copy each year. It goes without saying, they look forward to Ideals' arrival just around Christmas. They are great in their praise of such a beautiful and inspiring magazine instead of just a card. This is a wonderful way to express "hands across the sea."

Mrs. James McLachlan
Santa Cruz, California

The most beautiful Christmas gift I have received in a long time is Ideals. I have treasured this gift and each issue is very precious to me. I have thanked my friend Ellen Calnan a thousand times for a gift more valuable than gold.

Barbara A. Yageric
Williamsville, New York

I think your books are wonderful. My father was a teacher and subscribed to them all of my childhood. . . . Your books are one of the fondest memories from my childhood. As soon as the book arrived my sister and I would sit down and look at it together. I think that the contents of your books could put a little sunshine in everyone's life no matter what their age!

Kathy Bathe
St. Charles, Missouri

I really enjoy Ideals and always look forward to getting the next issue. Thanks for doing such a great job.

Kathleen M. King
Sarasota, Florida

Thanks for this beautiful magazine. I know God has blessed you by making it and surely He has blessed me by loving it.

Florence Beagle
Covington, Kentucky

For many years Ideals magazine has been my special gift to hospital patients and to others. They fill a special need for people.

Mrs. Carl H. Potratz
Waterloo, Indiana

* * *

Want to share your crafts and recipes? Readers are invited to submit original craft ideas and original recipes for possible development and publication in future *Ideals* issues. Please send recipes or query letters for craft ideas (with photograph, if possible) to Editorial Features Department, Ideals Publishing Corporation, P.O. Box 140300, Nashville, Tennessee 37214-0300. Please do not send craft samples; they cannot be returned.

Celebrating Life's Most Treasured Moments